AND I
COMPROMISED

AND I COMPROMISED

WHAT I AM NOW AND WHAT I HAVE NOW ARE NOT WHAT I HAD WANTED

Kandamaran. M

PARTRIDGE

A Penguin Random House Company

ISBN:	Hardcover	978-1-4828-4083-4
	Softcover	978-1-4828-4082-7
	eBook	978-1-4828-4081-0

Print information available on the last page.

To order additional copies of this book, contact
Partridge India
000 800 10062 62
orders.india@partridgepublishing.com

www.partridgepublishing.com/india

This book is dedicated to those who compromised on their dreams, passion and love.

Acknowledgments

This book isn't a single man's journey. There are a few beautiful and outstanding hearts that walked along with me behind the scenes.

The family comprising of Abhishek Mishra, Lotipa Mishra and Arpana Singh was one of the major backbones to make this book possible. The amount of patronage and advice I received from them is rarely earned in such a short span of time, and is visible in all the phases of this book.

Radhika – That's how I know her and would like to call her. She came out of nowhere to help me realize my dream. A Facebook chat, and later she willingly extended her hands to transform my thoughts into flowing words. I'm happy and glad that somewhere in my dream, she will be realizing her dream as well.

Bramma, Sivaram, Priscilla, Nitharshini and Freeda – Thank you for improving my insipid English, and encouraging me to tell my story to others.

My Family – They never failed to support me in every aspect of my life, including my remarkable new venture. I wish I could mention all your names here, but they have strictly set the word limit as 500.

Ramesh, Nithila, Sweatha and Preethi – Thank you for helping me out in designing the cover page.

Everyone has a Best Friend at different stages of his/her life. But some friends stay with you thick and thin through all these stages. Thank you, Raja Balachandran, Uma Balachandran, Timothy Jervis and every friend of mine for your support and valuable feedbacks.

YOU - If you are reading this, then you are one among the faithful hearts to whom I owe everything for picking up my book even after knowing that I am a debutant author.

Last but not the least, The Almighty. More than I, it was my family who offered prayers for me. I owe both of you for everything that I am today. Thank you for your abundant blessings.

AND I COMPROMISED

- *Cricket*   - *Movies/Media*   - *Politics*

I don't know what struck your mind first when you read these three words. But I believe that today, one can become popular, get rich and be a celebrity if he (no, I'm not a chauvinist) had made a career among any of the above.

It is said opportunity knocks your door once. But no one said that the door has to be opened for him to enter. For me, Mr. Opportunity has knocked on my door more than one time. If my responsibilities weren't in my way. I may have very well become famous for one of the things I have mentioned above.

All of us compromise something or the other every day, every minute and every second of our life. We don't realise it though because we think it's not important. Sometimes, we even pretend not to regret our choices. We only get to think of them with pleasure when we share those memories with others.

In the Indian context, the word compromise would mean making a choice that would allow you to

- Live up to society's standard of a successful man,
- fulfil the avowed dreams of your parents,
- accommodate the unsaid expectations of your girlfriend,
- secure the future of your siblings, and,
- Make yourself 'Presentable' in front of your in-laws,

- And well of course, squeeze in your passion, dream and love if you can after getting past all the above said qualifiers!

If you observe closely, there is only a thin line between Sacrifice and Compromise in that,

Sacrifice is something that you would choose to do. Whereas Compromise is something you are forced to do.

Before you fasten your seatbelts to begin the journey of "AND I COMPROMISED", I want you to know what made me an author.

Compromise is omnipresent in all our lives. Every passing moment is a compromise – knowingly or unknowingly! We may not even know it, but something or the other forces us to compromise on things on a daily basis.

But it's not the compromising part, nor the reason behind the same that seems to interest me. It's about what I realized and what kept me going even after I had compromised on the three most important things in my life.

I realized "LIFE ISN'T ABOUT WHAT YOU COULDN'T DO SO FAR, IT'S ABOUT WHAT YOU STILL CAN DO" This realization was also the fuel that ignited my desire to pen down this book.

My tryst with basketball

It was a typical tiring Thursday evening. I had been walking around the corner of a busy road, searching for the nearest ATM when I noticed a well-lit playground with a huge crowd vigorously cheering something or someone.

I managed to squeeze through the crowd and realised it was a basketball match between two local clubs. Pretty soon, the game and the fervent enthusiasm of the crowd had me completely engrossed. I decided to stand there and watch.

The sound of the ball rebounding from the backboard took me back a few years. . . Years ago when the thud thud of the ball had been my life. . . Years ago when the jingles of the hoop had been my music. . Years ago when I was representing my School in a Basketball Match.

It was the day my dad felt proud of me, the day he gave me my first gift, and the day my teammates hoisted me up on their shoulders after a historic win against Local school first after many years.

Yes, I was a junior state basketball player! It was my dream to be one and I've always loved the game.

My tryst with dance

It was the moment when my family first saw me on stage. A part of a huge crowd, my family was amused and proud to hear all the comments, cheers and applause coming my way from the audience.

When the event came to an end, everyone waited for the results to be announced as I held my breath for the same. At that exact moment, I missed the presence of a heart which was expecting me to lift the trophy

Everything around me seemed to hold still for a second as the judge announced the result: we had won the first place in the group dance event!

--- Yes, I'm a dancer, and it's my passion. ---

My tryst with love

I was randomly checking my emails one day when, fortunately or unfortunately, I happened to see a mail I had sent on 16th December.

I felt sick and very uneasy; for this was something I had never wanted to be reminded about for the rest of my life.

It was an email I had sent her; in fact, it was my last correspondence with her. The subject read: - "Don't Like To Mention the Subject!"

The mail dug up painful memories that I'd suppressed all these years.

--- Yes, I had loved her - truly, deeply and madly.

Those few compromises I made really mattered to me back then. Today, when I think about them, all I am left with are fond memories worth cherishing for a lifetime.

My tryst with basketball

There are certain things in your life that you tend to remember forever! And I'll surely remember this one for ages.

I was in the 6th grade and the summer holidays were in full swing! And my daily routine (as was the routine of everybody else on the team) started with an early morning practice session on the school grounds.

Summer holidays and early mornings rarely go together. But for me, it was different. I was up at 5.30 A.M., every single morning during the holidays in order to live my passion.

Being the son of the school's Physical Education Teacher had its advantages. I had the privilege of skipping the mandatory jog (3 rounds around the school grounds) that came before every warm-up session. And today, I was a tad excited as I picked up the basketball and accompanied the rest of the group as we gathered for the first round of the game. The reason? It was my first official try-out, which if successful, would earn me a place in the school's basketball team.

I (as well as everyone around me) had my apprehensions! Would I be able to make the shot? Would my aim be accurate? Would I even be able to touch the board? After all, I was way too young, too thin and too short (just 5 feet) to be basketball material! But something in me told that this was it, this was the moment I had been waiting for!

As I knelt down, touched the ground with my fingers and said my prayers, my mind raced back in time to when my father had let me in on the golden rule to scoring a basket, "If you want to convert it into a basket, aim for the square on the board".

His words rang continuously in my ears as I took up my position, glanced at the crowd standing in front of me, looked up at the square board which was my target that day, and slowly raised my hands; ready to shoot!

The warmth of the early morning sun hit my face, as if shouting, "You IDIOT! What are you waiting for? Go for it!" I took a deep breath ------ and released the ball from my hands, giving it just the right amount of pressure required to reach the square on the board.

The next thing I remember; I was searching for my dad in the crowd, hoping and wishing that he could have seen my first attempt; a successful shot! No wonder; my dad was standing near the long jump pit with a huge smile on his face. I knew then that he had seen me, and was quite happy that I had made it!

Of course, what could one lucky basket mean, you would ask? But I guess an angel was watching over me that day. I tried 10 more shots and scored a perfect 10/10. The next thing I knew, I was selected to represent my school's sub junior basketball team. No one would have believed it was possible except me and my dad who knew that I was blessed in some way!

AND I COMPROMISED

Fast forward a year! I was in the 7th grade. Despite getting selected to the team, I never actually 'played' a match. I was in the bench – substitute. A position which can be very exasperating as you keep waiting to replace an injured player. And finally that day came!

We were losing the sub junior district level match by a big margin and things were not any brighter when the coach decided to let me have a chance at the ball. Perhaps it was his way of making sure that every player had a chance to play before the game ended. But it was the silver lining in the dark cloud that I had been waiting for.

That was the first time I was entering a Basketball Court flushed with crowds. Not like those training sessions. I was facing real opponents. The gibberish chanting of the crowd; the fervent opponents; the hoops dangling on either sides. All these charged me up and nervousness was now a distant mirage.

First quarter of the game was completely dominated by them. We were yet to open our account and the team spirit was non-existent; let alone being low. Something had to be done to cheer it up. That something could only be the sight of the ball falling through the hoops!

The second quarter had started. I was playing as a point guard. From a defensive rebound we had the possession of the ball and we were advancing towards the opponent's hoop. In a quick chest pass, the ball had come into my possession. I was just out of the three-point line. And I shot!

There was no silence among the audience nor among the players. But for me time was suspended from the time the ball left the tip of my fingers. The ball hit millimetres above the square and it fell. Fell through the hoop all the way down the board! And that, was all what was needed.

And as they say, the rest was history! We indeed went on to lead and eventually win the game. My father was standing in the crowd, smiling, as the crowd cheered my team, and me! And I knew that that day those cheers meant more to him than they did to me!

That probably explained why I was included as one of the 5 main players representing my school in a district level basketball match the next year!

I really didn't know what it was that made me crazy about the game. But I really cherished every single time that I got to wear school jersey (my own jersey, complete with my name printed on the back) and represented my school in a match. And even though others took these matches as excuses to bunk Math classes and History tests, or take an entire day off, my love for the game was the only excuse I could even think of for my absence from school!

The attitude I developed on the court, the adrenaline rush before a game and the recognition I got at the end of it were the driving factors behind my transformation from a small, ignorant village boy to a basketball champ! And these were the same factors that made me get ready for one of the biggest games I had played in my entire life!

I was in the 9th grade, and we were taking part in the District Junior Level Championships. We were slotted to play against a local team notorious for its ace basketball players.

The odds were stacked against us like a huge mountain. The opponent team had some of the best basketball players in the district. We were just a budding team. We had never defeated them in our previous I-don't-know-how-many-attempts. Naturally, everyone was tense. Everyone; but me!

Attitude, you say? Not at all! I was more than happy to be a part of the 5 main players about to get on the court. And all through the journey to the venue, that was the only thing that filled my mind. Added to that was the fun we had while travelling to the venue (the fun you get every time while travelling to attend a competition).

We reached the venue by around 8.30 A.M., only to be utterly disappointed by the ground on which the game had to be played. Rather than a cement ground, the court was on a muddy track, with nothing but an old school board for company!

Luckily, our distaste for the court and its surroundings was shared by the coaches and referee who, after a brief discussion, decided to shift the venue back to my own school ground which happened to be the only decent ground available close by.

My happiness increased when I heard this, for we would be playing in local conditions and would have the support of the local crowd (aka my school friends)-just like our men in blue love playing on the spinning pitches of India.

The shift in venues delayed the game by an hour. While everyone was busy with something or the other, I went and sat beside the court with my teammates. Holding the basketball in my hands, my eyes were glued to the court as I listened to my teammates chattering away.

Someone walked onto the court and wrapped a new net around the ring. I still don't know what came over me that instant, because I stood up and walked on to the court, ball in hand. I angled the ball and made an attempt at a basket. It was a perfect shot! I turned around and attempted the basket on the other end of the court. Another successful attempt! Satisfied and felt blessed, I went back to the side-lines. And the game finally began!

Let me first brief you on the basics of how a basketball game usually starts. The tallest of the 5 players of both teams would stand in the middle of the court, with the remaining 4 players surrounding them on both sides. The referee would throw the ball up and both the players in the middle would jump, trying to tap it over to their team mates. Once that is done, the team mates would have to pass the ball among themselves and try to get a shot as they near the opposition team's net.

Like I said before, our opponent was a very strong team, and we were tense about it (tension started building up inside me at this point). But unknown to me, my teammates and coach had a secret weapon; ME!

I may be short, but I'm pretty quick for 5 feet. And that's the strategy my coach planned to utilize. The plan was simple. My teammates would try to pass the ball to me at every opportunity, and it would be my responsibility to convert those passes into shots.

We were counting on the fact that our rival team would not take me into consideration while playing, due to my height. After all, the saying goes that "When you are not ready to accept me, you will neither care about me nor follow me!"

The plan worked brilliantly! My teammate in the middle tapped the ball to another teammate as I ran to my shooting spot under the board. He in turn made a long pass to me and I went for it! The buzzer rang loud as the first shot of the game was scored, from our side! It all happened in less than 10 seconds!

We scored two more hoops in quick succession. More points followed as the ball came kept coming back to me and we executed our plan to perfection. We were cool and played confidently, like we had nothing to lose. Not like the other team though!

The local team was confused, tense and really irritated. It was the first time they were seeing a dirty score on their side of the board. They didn't know what hit them. By the time they realized that it was I who was scoring all those points, we had taken control of the game and were leading with a huge margin of nearly 30 points.

The last quarter of the game started, and we were leading 42-12. That's when the school bell went off for lunch. By this time, the entire school had come to know about our encounter with our rival team and that we were winning. That was enough to make everyone, from students and teachers to even the headmaster, to rush to the ground to witness the match. The headmaster was not complaining, and did not even try to stop the students from piling around the court. After all, it wasn't every day that a great team like MHSS stood a chance of losing to a juvenile team like ours.

The memories of that final quarter is still afresh like it happened an hour back.

The final whistle was about to sound and we were still leading comfortably. The ball was passed to me for one final shot. The crowd cheered me on, chanting my name in unison (just like you would hear the crowd chanting Dhoni, Dhoni, Dhoni ----- just before he faces the ball, and then cheer out loud when he makes that trademark 'Helicopter Shot'). I grabbed the ball, dashed towards the hoop and made one last (and really stylish) attempt. The ball sailed through the net beautifully; a perfect shot!

The final whistle blew, signalling the end of the game! The scoreboard read 72-23. We had won! A great and a historic win against MHSS! Before the realization could sink in, the entire crowd swarmed the court, cheering me on as I was hoisted by my teammates. At that moment, my pleasure (of winning the game) and happiness (for being recognized) knew no bounds!

Fast forward to present day! When I think about my basketball days now, that was the first and the last thing I remember about the game. For as I reached the 10th grade, I had to compromise my dream and concentrate only on my studies. And If you were in my place (and in a country like India), you would know what I mean!

After passing the 10th, I was asked (or rather made) to join the Biology stream. My parents wanted me to study for the Bachelor of Dental science (BDS) degree, for it was their dream that I become a dentist. But I had different ideas of my own. I learnt from one of my dad's students that if I played basketball well enough, I would easily get hired by government sector banks like the IOB. And considering the fact that I was frequently called to play for the local clubs, I knew that if I played for these banks, one of them would surely want me to stick around with them, thereby offering me a job. It was just like the Ranji Trophy in Cricket. And I congratulated myself on coming up with a brilliant 'Wah, What an idea sir ji' moment.

This particular thought made me lose interest in my studies as I knew I would get a job anyways. With that, you can pretty much guess what my 12th board score would have been. And I wasn't the least bit surprised when the result came as 'Average'. As if nothing significant had happened, I started my basketball practice sessions after the holidays.

Considering my marks, I was sure that I would have to join a college in the sports quota and so, applied for a seat in Loyola College, Chennai, and waited eagerly for the results.

To this day, I don't understand why my parents forced me to join an Arts College in my local town itself, and how the hell I was coaxed into joining it. Worse, I had to take a subject I was least interested in Commerce.

That's right! My parents made me compromise my dreams by saying that Commerce graduates have a great future and that I could easily do PG, M.Com, CA and what not after I completed my graduation!

There was little room or opportunity for me to open my mouth to voice my feelings about this entire arrangement. They had said it, and it was done! And I did not realize that I had become a Commerce student until the day my elder sister aka my schoolmate, aka my college senior took me to the college and introduced me to my new classmates.

B.Com, M.Com, CA….. Where could I possibly squeeze basketball in all this? And as a basketball player who still loves the game even today after so many years, I really wondered that day as to where my life would lead me!

My thoughts scattered as the crowd in whose midst I was standing, erupted in cheers suddenly. The match between the local clubs was over, and one of the teams had earned a historic victory over the other.

'Time for me to leave and get back into the humdrum of daily life', I thought as I tried to move away from the crowd. That's when I noticed something.

A man and woman were hugging a boy, probably their son, for winning the match. At the same time, at the other end of the court, another man and woman were trying to console their son by saying that it was just not his day.

At that moment, I realized that it wouldn't take long for me and my wife to step into the shoes of these parents (I knew would marry eventually) who were praising and consoling their respective children. I pictured myself and my wife doing the same thing to my son (I'm not a chauvinist), and decided then and there that my son would definitely get all the things in life he wanted, all the things I missed out on!

As these thoughts ran through my mind, I started walking back home. And that's when I started recollecting what had happened to me after I became a so called Bachelor of commerce student.

It took me a whole semester to accept the fact that I was indeed going to be a B.Com graduate. There was no running away from it, or trying to erase it from my thoughts. That was what I was going to be eventually. I started writing my name followed by B.Com, M.Com, and CA in every piece of paper I could get my hands on in order to reassure myself that like everything else, this too, had happened for a reason. But nightmares of becoming nothing in life but a professor or Chartered Accountant haunted me day and night.

And that's when I guess the goddess Sarasvati decided to bless me again.

After finishing college one day, I happened to be sitting in the institution's basketball court, cherishing my memories as a basketball player, when I noticed a group of students dancing in the open air auditorium located right next to the court. I got up and asked some seniors standing nearby as to what was going on.

My seniors informed me that it was the Fine Arts team practicing for some competition. I felt a breeze of fresh air hit my face as I realized that my life in this college was not over, not yet!

One of my seniors (my basketball mate as well) introduced me to the Fine Arts team, and the rest as they say is history! My tryst with dance began from there, and what followed was a new chapter in my life filled with a new passion and dream, and a new compromise.

Oh, and did I forget to tell you though that I was not completely new to dancing? I had been dancing for the annual day function of my school every year from my pre-primary years. So dance was not new for me here. But the experience I am about to narrate was!

My tryst with dance

School and college years must have been fun for almost every one of us. And I bet nearly everyone would have loads of memories about those days to cherish even now. And while the quintessential college grad would reminiscence about his buddies, the girls and of course, about the teachers, I could and can still remember only one thing about my college days; my own way of having fun; the Dancing Way!

The first year of college saw me as one of the members in the official dance team. By the 2nd year, I had been promoted as the lead dancer for the team. And by the 3rd year, I had been given the ultimate task of heading the entire college dance team during cultural shows and intercollegiate events.

I am from a quintessential Indian family, which means like everybody else, I faced my share of restrictions and discouragements from family members who looked down upon dancers, singers and every other person with a possible connection to the media field.

Even the occasional support from close relatives was looked down upon with disdain, and you can possibly imagine a Kargil war like scenario at home whenever the topic of my interest in dance came up.

Like a good Indian student, I was asked to complete my studies without any arrears, graduate with flying colours, get a well-paid job and settle down in life as soon as possible. To this day, I repeat the excuses to myself, saying that "My parents are too orthodox, and would not want their kid to be in the media business."

It was for this very reason as well (and the aforementioned Kargil situation) that I decided to not let my parents know about my tryst with dance during my college days. As I started winning college competitions and the hearts of the people who watched me dance, my interest turned to a passion of sorts. And I knew that Mother Saraswathi had blessed me in more ways than one.

The fame and recognition I received for my dancing skills in my town prompted me to do something different.

It was during the 3rd semester of my college that a friend of mine decided to open a Dance School; the first of its kind in my town. I decided to join hands with my friend and establish myself as a professional dancer. And unknown to my family members who thought that their son was dutifully attending college; I started traveling to different districts to participate in several dance competitions.

My parents never complained about my late night schedules and long absences from home, even though I was caught telling the same lie on more than one occasion. I attribute their silence to the fact that till then, I had never failed an exam in my college and was literally 'arrear-free'.

AND I COMPROMISED

Everything went according to plan. Days flew by quickly, my college days were coming to an end, dance had firmly rooted itself as a passion in my heart, and I was spending every other minute of my time and energy on it. And then entered the anti-hero who finds his way into every single success story out there. In my case, it was a Checkmate situation out of which I could not escape!

I was called to audition for a major dance competition, the winner of which would get a world trip contract for 2 years! I was super excited. Here was a chance to prove to the world that I was a dancer!

The auditions were held in another town. And like every other occasion, I had to tell a lie to my parents in order to participate. I took the risk and travelled to the location, eager to show my mettle. 1st Round – I sailed through. 2nd Round: Selected again. And the final round? In Mumbai they said!

My world literally came crashing down at my feet when I heard that the final auditions would be held in Mumbai. 'Bullshit!' I thought. How the hell was I supposed to travel several miles to a distant location without my parents knowing about it? And how in the world would I be able to survive in Mumbai for those 4 days of the final audition without any money?

I decided to open my heart to my parents, and try to make them understand that a really big Mr. Opportunity was knocking at my door right then. I expected them to understand. But boy was I wrong!

It wasn't a Kargil War effect this time, but more along the lines of Hiroshima and Nagasaki. My parents were really shocked to learn of my secret dance rendezvous (I had to tell them about all my dance related activities, including the lies I had told, in order to persuade them that I was actually good at dancing). And they were aghast to find out that I actually planned to travel to Mumbai for the final auditions when my final semester exams were falling on the same dates as the former. Throughout their laments, my parents had only one thing to point out; if I travelled to Mumbai, I would miss my exams, and eventually, my college degree. And that was something they would not hear of at all! Boy did I wish I had some arrears at that instant!

I pleaded, I cajoled, I cried, but it was no use. I could not justify the risk I was taking to fulfil my passion. And there was no way they were going to accept the fact that the risk their son was about to take could possibly spell great success for him in a different field in the near future.

You could possibly guess what happened next. I was placed under house arrest and was subjected to varying degrees of emotional blackmail (again a quintessential Indian tool to get what you want). All of this resulted in my missing the final auditions, quitting the competition, and quitting the dance school I had come to love.

Hold on! I'm not finished yet! For here comes the sudden twist in a climax that was already overburdened with my heavy heart.

After the altercation with my parents, I chose to stay at home for 2 weeks and prepare for my final semester exams which were to be held on the 24th of July (the same day as the dance auditions in Mumbai). Just 2 days before the exams, I went to my college to collect my hall ticket. I met my friends and casually chatted with them for some time. By the time I returned home in the evening, I was feeling a bit sick. I attributed it to being upset over the fact that I had missed out on the auditions, and had literally kicked Mr. Opportunity right out of the front door.

By night, I was feeling worse. And that's when I noticed it. A small reddish bump, similar to a heat boil on my right arm. I thought I would sleep it off, but woke up the next morning, covered from head to toe by those boils. I was rushed to the doctor who conveniently labelled it, "CHICKEN POX".

And that's how my compromise ended that day! I didn't go to the auditions; I missed out on my semester exams as well, and was bed ridden for an entire week with some really painful boils. But more than my body and mind, it was my heart that ached the worst that day! And more than the hurt of being affected by chicken pox or missing out on my final semester exams, the thought of missing out on a potentially life changing event which could have made my dreams come true, was what broke my heart that day!

Now tell me! Did I really need to compromise?

Six months of idleness, sitting at home and preparing for that last final semester literally made me scream out in frustration. It was then that I decided to do something with my life.

The call-centre industry was at its peak in those days. And there were plenty of openings for interested candidates. I decided to go to Chennai with the intent of joining one of these call centres. Winning over my parent's approval was not that easy. But this time, I had a stronghold in the form of my uncle who promised to help me, on one condition. That I remain unique! His words ring in my ears to this day, "Wherever you go, I can't and don't want to see you as one among the common public. You should stand out in everything you do, and prove your worth on every occasion."

With that promise guaranteed from me, he placed Rs. 1500 in my hands, and sent me off on a bus to Chennai that night. And that's where a major diversion in my career took place; from a state level basketball player to a call centre employee for a US based networking client.

Throughout the journey my mind kept wandering back to one thing; my tryst with different passions and how I had to compromise something every time I fell in love with it. Starting as a basketball player, I traced my life past the B.com graduate and dancer to what I was about to be today, a call centre employee. And through this journey, I had come to realize that if I started to like or love something, it would never stay with me and eventually leave me heartbroken.

And so, starting work at the company the next day, I made a solemn promise never to think of basketball, B.Com or dance ever again, let alone practice any of them. As for the events that led to me getting the job in a call centre; I decided to ignore that page of my journey!

I don't think experiences are different from anyone else working night shifts in a call-centre. Sleeping in purposefully darkened rooms (we sleep during the day remember?), insurmountable work pressure, fun on weekends, frequent team outings, less frequent onsite visits, office grapevines… you name it! I experienced all the things that any other night shift employee in a call centre would have experienced, and would still be experiencing every day.

Three idle years went by with me doing the same job over and over again. And then, one fine day, it happened. A new twist in my life, a breath of fresh air and possibly, the beginning of a new chapter in the story 'And I Compromised'. And all this happened because over the course of these three years, I had never told my colleagues that I was a dancer.

One fine night, we (my team) were invited to a party in one of the most happening pubs in the city. We were a total of 10 colleagues and the pub had a huge dance floor that could easily accommodate us all and many more dancers as well.

Being a non-smoker and a non-drinker (that was a long time ago, folks!), I resorted to eating the side dishes that my colleagues ordered with their drinks (I bet there is at least one guy in every gang out there who forces his friends to spend more on the side dishes than on the liquor that they drink!).

Full and bored (you would be too if you happen to end up in a group where everyone except you drinks), I invited myself on to the dance floor for a few quick moves. That was the first day my colleagues actually witnessed me dancing. Needless to say, they were awestruck! Not just because of moves I had shown but because of the fact that I got to dance with the prettiest girl in the crowd who was mighty impressed with my slick moves.

That night was one of the most memorable nights I had had in a while. And I went home a happy man that day. Not because I had danced with the prettiest girl in the crowd, but because I had danced! After a very long time, I had danced.

By the time I reached the office the next day, the grapevine was abuzz with rumours of how I had danced and impressed a really hot girl to the extent that she had invited me to spend the night with her. On that day, I realized the true essence of an office grapevine and its life altering effects on employees in the corporate world.

I knew I had been noticed for my dance that night. Therefore, it didn't come as a surprise to me when I came to know that, I had been nominated to dance in an office function the next week. Having felt extremely liberated after dancing to my heart's content that night, I decided to give it another go. For, as you and I both know, dance had been everything to me at one point of time.

But I didn't feel the excitement that I normally felt when I danced. This time, I was really nervous. And I had never ever felt like this at any part of my dance journey. I had performed on many stages, had seen huge crowds! But that day, I was feeling extremely nervous to perform on stage in front of my colleagues.

I had decided to dance for a fusion number (a mixture of western and local songs) for the duration of the 4 minutes that was allotted to me. It was a sequence I already knew, so I let go of all my apprehensions, cleared my mind to think straight, and got ready to shake my legs.

At this point, I would like to point out a slight advantage I had and still have over several other dancers out there. I always smile when I dance. And I don't just smile. I make it a point to maintain eye contact with the crowd constantly, smiling at them while I dance, so that my expressions would overpower their minds, and they would start enjoying my moves.

My name was announced and I made it a point to enter as soon as the song began. My first step? A back flip and a stunt, standing upside down on one hand for about 3 seconds!

The entire crowd went mad as soon as they saw my entry. And there was no stopping after that – Neither the crowd nor me.

The first song which was filled with plenty of stylish moves and attention grabbing steps left me exhausted. So I faked the second song by doing some simple interactive steps along with the crowd as I prepared myself mentally and physically for the third and final song in the sequence.

The third song started and I started dancing again. There was a line in the final song that went something like this (in the local language) "I started dreaming even when my eyes are open, and that's cause of YOU".

My original intention was to move to the side of the stage where the majority of girls were seated, and imitate line by pointing my fingers at them. Lord knows why, on the spur of the moment, I decided to move to the opposite side of the stage where the boys were seated. My fingers rose in the air and pointed out a girl who was sitting by herself, all alone in a big crowd of boys.

The crowd went berserk at my move yet again. And by the time they settled down in their seats, the performance was over!

What followed of course was expected. I was hugged, appreciated and congratulated for my performance. By the way, don't think I am blowing my own trumpet. If you remember, this is my book. And I have every right to spice up my stories a bit!

So by now, I knew I must have impressed the pretty girl I had pointed to during my dance performance. I took this as the perfect opportunity to start a casual conversation. And that's when I heard from someone that this was her first day in the company, and that she had just started training for a pilot project.

Just imagine how she must have felt when someone she had never seen before pointed out to her in front of all those people, that too on the very first day of her joining the company. Embarrassing!

Deeply embarrassed myself, I started searching for a way to convey my apologies to her, knowing that I would have definitely offended her. But I missed her that day!

The next two days being my weekend, I experienced something I had never experienced before. A mad rush to go to office the first thing on Monday night. I don't know what made me feel this way. But I was really waiting for Monday night to arrive.

Alas! Luck did not favour me then, as while I was heading a nesting team of new employees, I heard she was put in another project. This made it nearly impossible for me to meet her except the time when she used to come out of the training room for dinner or for short breaks.

We used to walk past each other and exchange glances during these brief visits. And I must admit that, more than coincidence, I managed to arrange a few of these situations myself, and purposely walk past her, but fake that I had come by casually.

Although given the opportunity on more than one of these brief visits, my efforts to start a conversation with her proved to be fruitless, and all I managed to do was make eye contact with her and smile as we passed each other. And I must admit, her smile literally passed an electric current through my body every time I saw it.

A week passed by like this; both of us just staring at each other as we walked past each other. The day arrived when I had to go on my ten day annual break. I desperately wanted to speak to her before leaving for my break, and decided to do so that day itself.

I opted to wait for her near the parking area, and sat on the steps, waiting for her. And then she came! Trust me when I say that at that moment, I did not have the courage to even stand up and introduce myself, let alone say that I was sorry for the other day.

She just simply crossed me, giving me a side long glance and that infectious smile again, as she left the office. It was a good feeling, and I decided to let it continue. I left town for the holidays, not thinking about (minding would be a better word here) missing her for those ten days.

With so many expectations, I eagerly returned to office after my break, waiting to see her. To be honest, I didn't miss her at all during those ten days because there were so many other things keeping my mind preoccupied during my vacation. But while travelling back, throughout the journey, the thought of seeing her again kept my mind happy and my adrenalin levels rushing uncontrollably.

I got ready for office with extra vigour that day. It was a beautiful morning, the air was fresh, the day was bright, the weather was cool, and everything I saw looked new and interesting. Did I forget to mention the songs that were playing in my car while I drove to work? Yup ---- it looked like a day that was tailor made for me!

That was probably when I realized something new brewing inside me, an uneasy and yet blissful feeling about a possible relationship between us (even though both of us did not know a thing about each other save for a few glances now and then).

Call it my luck or fate, but what I was expecting didn't happen. I was not able to spot her in any of the usual break timings. But I was not one to back down that easily. There are plenty of resources in every office to know about someone, especially if that someone happens to be a girl. In my case, my resources informed me that she had finished training and had moved on to the floor to start working.

I decided to meet her during dinner break in the cafeteria. I took a friend along (rather, dragged him along) with me, giving him a fake excuse that I was very hungry. I was expecting to meet her there, and the gods finally decided to smile on me.

There she was, sitting at a table with her friends, having her dinner as she casually chatted with them over something. My heart took a leap the moment I saw her. She was so beautiful. And at that moment, everything else around me blurred so that my heart and mind could focus only on her (amazing, considering the fact that the heart never listens to the brain and vice versa when you are in love).

I forcibly restrained myself from walking over to the table and introducing myself. Rather, I occupied the table right opposite hers so as to have a straight view. I looked at her and smiled, expecting her to smile back. She looked at me, and then looked away, and that was that. No smile, no eyes lighting up like mine did. She just looked away as if she had never seen me before. 'How rude!' I thought.

I left the cafeteria and headed back to my work desk, sad and disheartened. It will probably be at times like these that your friends tend to cheer you up with suggestions and examples of what to do at a time like this. Their words would seriously make you think that the girl you are pursuing was born just for you. My friend did just that for me that day, and I felt really glad, more so because of the fact that I was hoping to hear such words from someone.

He insisted that I drop her a mail and gauge her response. After hesitating for what felt like a million years, I decided to do so and started my first ever conversation with her. This is pretty much how it went.

AND I COMPROMISED

Me: Hi, how are you and do you recognize me?

Her: I'm sorry. I don't recognize you!!

Me (I was more disheartened that she didn't even recognize me, but decided to continue anyway): I pointed out at you in the huge crowd when I danced that day.

Her: Oh yeah, I know you. I'm sorry I didn't know your name and so couldn't recognize you. Btw, I wanted to tell you that you danced great that day and your moves were just awesome.

Oooooooooooh Yeah! What else would you want after hearing such a compliment from the person you think is your sweetheart? I flew up to cloud 9 that instant, and would have literally jumped up and down at my desk in joy had it not been for the conversation that was still going on. She was waiting for a response and I took this as the right chance to start a new relationship. The first impression is always the best impression they say, and I made sure my first impression lasted with her for days to come.

Our email conversations slowly increased and led to SMS chats, which in turn led to overnight calls. And you probably know what happened next. I started spending entire days, nights, spring, summer, autumn and winter thinking about her. My feelings for her had developed into a relationship I could not exactly name. It was definitely not friendship, but something more than that for me. For her, I was a very close, very special friend. At a point of time, we had shared almost every little detail about ourselves to each other.

At this time, I believe it would be appropriate if I let you know few things about her. I have described these details in the present tense as I believe that she would still be the same in these aspects.

She is a native of Mumbai. She loves the colours purple, black and white. Like every other girl, she is crazy about chocolates. She has a very strong belief in God, never failing to visit the temple every Thursday. She loves BMW cars and goes bonkers whenever she sees one on the road. She loves to watch movies (we used to watch back to back movies sometimes).

She hates the smell of alcohol and cigarette smoke, not to mention anyone who smokes or drinks as well. She is her Dad's princess and excelled in her studies, especially Mathematics (she secured 2nd rank in her university). And to top it all off, she is a big time foodie and loves chaat-food, never hesitating to stop by a chaat street if we happened to cross one.

On to the main track, most of the time, we used to end up meeting at a pizza or Marry Brown restaurant. If not that, then a movie and if not that as well, we would just opt for a long walk. In fact, we used to walk for hours every day after work. This was pretty much how the first two months of our relationship flew by.

We used to give a wakeup call to each other every day in order to get ready for work in time. And we always made it a point to have a long talk every night before hitting the bed. It pretty much grew to the extent that my day did not start or end without talking to her, pretty much like how the earth does not wake up or go to sleep without the sunrise or the sunset. Not one of those 60 days went by without me speaking to her and vice versa. And then something came along that made us actually realize how much we cared for and missed each other, something that brought us miles closer.

After spending nearly 3 years in the organization, my office decided to send me for an onsite visit to meet a client. It was a visit to the USA for a couple of months, and I had waited for this opportunity for a very long time, in fact from the time I joined the company. I was obviously overjoyed at the prospect of finally cracking it and going abroad.

With just a week left for my trip, both of us planned our schedule in accordance with that one week. Most of the days flew by in shopping for the journey. But just two days before I left, I decided to give her something, a surprise that would remain etched in her memory till I come back.

I decided to buy her a watch (the Purple Mania collection from Titan, keeping in mind that she adores anything and everything purple). I also got a basket of chocolates and a diary in which I wrote everything that had happened between us from day one till then, including all those long night chats and phone calls; and all the fun we had had in those few months. I planned to write it like a story to make it more impressive.

Now came the difficult part. I didn't just want to hand these gifts to her and shout 'SURPRISE'. Rather, I wanted her to find them herself. And the best way to do that was to hide them in her room without her knowledge. I would not be able to do that, with her staying in a ladies hostel. But I knew someone who would; her roommate! But could this be possible?

Luckily, it was. And lady luck seemed to favour me that day. I was thinking of how to contact her roommate when I called her. She told me she would be going for a bath and would be keeping her mobile phone connected to the charger. I took this as the perfect opportunity to contact her roommate. I called her phone again, hoping, praying that her roommate would pick up the call as I knew that she had already left for her bath.

I was happy, and genuinely surprised when her roommate picked up the phone and asked me to call later as my girl had gone to the restroom. I literally screamed into her ear that I wanted to speak to her and not my girl, even before she could finish saying what she wanted to say. This made her stop and listen to me attentively. I asked her to come down to the mobile shop located near her hostel within the next 5 minutes. I told her of my surprise gifts and how I wanted to surprise her before leaving for California.

Till today, I can't recollect how I managed to reach that mobile shop in 5 minutes. All I know was that I made it with time to spare. Her roommate came down and we introduced ourselves formally, this being our first meeting. I explained my plan to her in detail, including the gifts I had got for my girl. I asked her to hide the three gifts in different places in her room and to let me know where she had hidden them. I also asked her to let me know the dress colour my girl was wearing when she came out of the shower.

It was time to execute the plan. I started back with bated breath, praying that all went well. By the time I reached my room, I had received a message from her roommate telling me where she had hidden the gift and what colour dress my girl was wearing. Operation Surprise had started!

I called her and started chatting with her casually. At one point of time, I remarked that I could guess the colour of the dress that she was wearing that instant. She laughed and replied that I could never find out. I revealed the colour and could immediately gauge her reaction. She was shell shocked and started looking out her room window to see if I was looking at her from somewhere on the road below.

To keep the surprises coming, I asked her to walk over to the bookshelf nearby and search for something just behind the book titled 'The Three Mistakes of My Life' by Chetan Bhagat. She walked over and did what I asked her to do, and found the watch hiding behind the book.

She was utterly baffled, and I could judge it by the way she remained silent on the phone as she opened the box. I had also asked her roommate to take a video of her reactions as she found these gifts one after the other. When she opened the box and found the purple colour watch in it, her happiness knew no bounds.

But it didn't stop there, and I didn't want it to. I asked her to open her black colored travel bag that she usually keep underneath her bed. She asked me why? as she pulled the bag out and searched below the black color dress just like I instructed her to. That's when she found my second gift, a box full of 'Hershey's Kisses' Chocolates.

I could tell by now that she had started tearing up. But before the kajal on her gorgeous eyes got washed away completely, I instructed her to sit down, take the pillow and keep it on her lap. She did and saw the third and last gift, the diary in which I had written about her and the beautiful moments we had shared during those 60 days. And that was that! She started crying uncontrollably as she picked up the diary and read few pages;

The story of how a village boy came to Chennai and slowly fell in love with a girl from Mumbai.

Yes! I had started loving her; truly, madly and deeply.

AND I COMPROMISED

The date of my onsite visit was just a day before Valentine's Day. I had a thought that this might be the perfect time to propose to her, but stopped myself from doing so. Because according to her, I was just her best friend.

My onsite visit to USA stretched on for three months. Those three months brought us closer together. God knows what would have happened to us if someone had not invented social networks like FB and Skype!

She even cried on more than a few occasions, claiming to miss me very badly. Those tears disturbed me very much. I had many friends apart from her, even some who were closer to me than her. But nobody had cried for me like she did. No, they were more interested in what I would be buying for them and often took the liberty of ordering as many items as they wanted. But that's what friends would normally do, right? So what was this relationship between us that made her cry out for me? Maybe it was something different. 'Maybe a long term commitment', I thought.

I never asked her why she felt like that about me. Nor did I feel worried about her thoughts. A few email conversations between us even had her mentioning how much the trip and my absence had made her realize the extent she cared for me and what I actually meant to her.

Her words gave me the confidence to take the relationship to the next level. I decided I would ask her the same question every man asks his life partner; 'will you marry me'? I decided I would pop the question the moment I arrived back in town. The thought kept running over and over in my mind, and I decided to surprise her big time when I arrived. If I could plan a surprise for her on such short notice before leaving for my onsite visit, surely I would be able to do something bigger with better planning. I knew she had enjoyed the previous surprise when I saw the video of her getting those gifts. I decided to go for it and plan a really huge surprise for her on the day I would ask her to marry me.

Her birthday falls on June 15th, and I made up my mind to give her a day she could never imagine, and would never be able to forget in her life.

If I think about it now, the 3 months of onsite visit breezed past me like 3 days. However, back then, it was more like 3 agonizing years. Why? Because I was in love!

I finally arrived back in Chennai by the end of May, and went to meet her. By now, you would have guessed that I didn't visit her empty-handed. No I didn't. I made it a point to get her an iPod and a bag full of imported chocolates. She was mighty glad that I was back.

I had also bought other smaller items which I planned to gift her on her birthday. And my surprise for her started with me leaving for my hometown just 3 days before her birthday. She was sad, but let me go anyway after I convinced her that I would be back for her birthday.

It was the evening of June 13th. I called her as usual just before she left for office for the day. I kept my voice sober and very sorrowful, and revealed that due to unavoidable circumstances, I would not be able to make it for her birthday.

The disappointment in her voice was immediate. She sounded very dull when she claimed that more than being there for her birthday, it was good that I had some extra time to spend with my family. She felt my, being with my family was more important than celebrating her birthday with her. But it was very obvious that the words were only coming from her mouth, and not from her heart.

That very night, I started to Chennai without informing her. 10 hours of straight travel. She called me during all her breaks and I spoke to her as if nothing had happened. Poor girl, she did not even have a clue that I was on my way to see her.

14th June: A day before her birthday. I reached the city early in the morning (somewhere between 5.45 – 6.00 a.m.), rushed home to freshen up, and headed over to my pick up point exactly on time. She had just finished her shift and had started walking back to her hostel. I called her from across the road, not telling her that I was there. Rather, I kept the conversation casual and commented that I could guess what colour dress she was wearing then. She complained that I must be cheating, for there was no way I could guess it correctly every time.

As she was about to cross the road (she was on the phone with me the whole time), I crossed the other half of the road and came to a stop right in front of her. A wild scream emanated from her lips, causing at least a dozen or more bystanders to look at us in alarm and her face to go a deep beetroot red. But that wasn't all. Without hesitating a second, she hugged me right there in the middle of the road!

The realisation of my actually being there in front of her took some time to sink in and the tears that flowed freely from her eyes more than clearly revealed her happiness at my presence on her birthday; in her life. According to her, the celebrations had already started!

We enjoyed our daily walk (after her shift ended) till her hostel. But this time, everything about it was different from all those other days. It was still very early in the morning, about 6.30 a.m. or so. The sun was late today and the day was a bit gloomy.

A very cool breeze blew past us, carrying with it the sweet fragrances of flowers. It was silent all around, save the occasional chirping of birds high up on the branches of the trees above our heads, the sweeping sound made by a servant outside a house and the milkman ringing the bell as he drove past us.

What's so different in this you ask? Well it was the way we walked that day that was so different from all the other days. Holding hands gently, her head nestling on my shoulder and my other hand holding her hip gently from behind.

AND I COMPROMISED

We walked slowly, hand in hand in that dim morning light, chatting about my surprise visit. I can still remember that day as if it had happened yesterday. And if ever there had been a moment where I had lived my life fully, that was it.

After the really romantic walk, I had asked her to join me for lunch. She refused immediately, saying she needed to rest and had already made plans to go shopping with her roommate for her birthday. But I knew her too much to take the reply at face value. If she said no, she really meant yes. And more than any other day, that day I knew that's what she meant, and wanted. And by revealing her plans to me, she had indirectly asked me to take her shopping later in the day.

I wanted to make her believe that I had spent all my savings in my hometown, and did not have any money to spend on her birthday. I waited for the right moment to strike up the conversation when she started it herself, by thanking me for being there for her birthday since she had thought I would not make it.

I took this as the right moment to talk to her, and asked, 'Hey Liz, why don't you make a wish that I can buy for your birthday? I swear I will get it for you pretty soon'.

She didn't reply immediately, but took my hand in hers and gave a gentle kiss. She then responded by saying that my presence felt more to her than anything, and was more than anything she could ever wish for.

With a smile on my face, I replied 'This is the first birthday I am going to spend with you. And I really want to make it very special. So make a wish.'

She never made a wish, but I did. And my wish was to keep surprising her from 12've to 12've.

I started by creating a scene about overshooting my expenses in my hometown, stating that as a result, I would not be able to buy her anything the next day. But she didn't seem worried about that at all. All she wanted me to do was to be the first person to wish her on her birthday. And that she said would be more than enough.

AND I COMPROMISED

I sketched a plan for our rendezvous.

- A movie at noon
- A sumptuous lunch
- Birthday shopping
- Dinner at, MURUGAN IDLY SHOP (her favorite place. She loved the mouth-watering idlies served there, not to mention the different coloured chutneys)

So this was our plan or rather what she thought was the plan. She was as excited as I was, to spend the day together.

According to the plan, I would return home as soon as I dropped her at the hostel. But I had my own plans. I intended to celebrate her birthday like never before. And I know the few weirdoes (like me) reading this will surely wear a smile of recognition.

I had booked movie tickets for a 4.00 p.m. show. It was a 2 hour movie but we hardly noticed the time, or the screen. Now don't go about getting all kinds of wrong ideas about what couples who don't watch movies in the theatres but still visit them, do. All I intended to do at that moment was put to another one of my surprise plans into action.

With my miser act working out better than I had planned, we went shopping for her birthday, and selected a dress for her. It was a Maroon and white colour combination, and complimented her very nicely, although she was more intent on buying a purpled coloured one.

By the time I dropped her at the hostel, it was 8.30 p.m. I asked her to get ready in twenty minutes and that I would pick her up for dinner in an auto. Only that the auto turned out to be something with 4 wheels and a fantastic symbol on the front.

Surprise 1: As I mentioned before, she was crazy about BMWs. So I went straight to a car rental service to pick one up for the night. According to her, I was coming by auto to pick her up.

Surprise 2: Her love for chocolates can paralleled only by her love for flowers. So undoubtedly they were a part of my cast crew for the surprise script.

Surprise 3: I went straight to a 5 star hotel to arrange a candle-night dinner for us. The hotel supervisor advised against ordering a cake as the hotel would serve one as a complimentary offer. And so this is the Murugan Idli shop that I was taking her to!

With every little detail of the surprise arranged perfectly, I called her up just before I started from the hotel and told her that I would be there in a few minutes to pick her up 'in auto'.

She replied saying that she was almost ready, and asked me to give her a missed call once I reached the hostel. No sooner than I messaged her that she came down. That, in fact, was a HUGE surprise for me.

AND I COMPROMISED

I sat inside the car, watching her as she came out of the hostel and started searching for the auto I was in. She called me up and said she could not find me anywhere. I asked her to walk further down the street.

As she started walking down the street, she said over the phone "You know what? There is a BMW parked in this street".

I asked her whether she was talking about the BMW with the parking lights on. She responded "Yes", and started searching for me. I could see her getting anxious now. She asked where I was again.

As she reached the car, I asked her "Did the door of that BMW car opened just now?"

Her reply trailed off midway even as it was a monosyllable – "Yes" - as she looked into the car and gasped! And then, there was a long pause!

I climbed out of the car like a reel life hero and quipped "Hey, what's up? Why don't you pop in?" All that came out of her mouth was a meek squeak. And her silence continued until we started moving.

I looked at her to notice that she had closed her mouth with her hands and the same reaction she had had on her face when she had seen the purple watch was again there; so this was the first of the birthday gifts I presented her. I enjoyed her reaction to the core and acted normally, as if whatever was happening was no big deal at all.

We went for a small drive near the beach, and I switched on her favourite music track. I could see that she was mentally preparing herself to expect more surprises, and was possibly wondering, "what is this guy going to do next?'

After a few minutes of thinking, she couldn't hold it in her any longer and asked me "Kiddo, what's happening and where are we heading?" (Yeah, she used to call me by that name). And that was the first and the last time that she actually asked me that question.

I replied that we were heading to Murugan Idly Shop for dinner as I had booked a table for us there. She squealed in delight at the prospect of visiting the restaurant in a BMW car. And I smiled to myself, silently enjoying her innocent expressions and thinking "Poor girl" as the car silently entered the 5 star hotel. Her eyes widened as she gaped at the hotel, awestruck at where we had stopped.

I gave the key to the valet as we entered the hotel. She was immediately welcomed by four gorgeous receptionists with beautiful flowers. () As she received the flowers from the receptionist, all she could do was squeeze my hand tightly and ask "What's happening here?"

We got into the lift to the restaurant. And as we moved up, I moved closer to her and whispered, ever so softly in her ear "It's a sweet birthday celebration for my princess".

AND I COMPROMISED

She nudged my shoulder kiddingly "My Princess? Stop it Kiddo!"

The restaurant was located on the rooftop. And as we entered it, I could see the surprise on her face, but could also feel the same expression developing on my face as well. As the supervisor welcomed and guided us to the table I had booked earlier, I kept wondering if the emphasis was on "My" or "Princess".

My thoughts were quickly placed on the backburner though, as we started our dinner. With just 20 minutes left for midnight, she received a call from her parents. It was her mom and she revealed that she had come out for dinner with me. And contrary to other moms who would usually fuss or throw a tantrum when they know their daughters were out with someone so late in the night, her mom simply instructed her to reach home early and safe. 'Lucky me', I thought.

With just 5 minutes left for midnight, the waiter started clearing our table. As she started wondering why, came the moment I had been waiting for all night.

The waiters placed a huge birthday cake on our table, along with all the gifts I had bought for her. As I lit the birthday candles, I could see her eyes welling up with tears which she had no intention of wiping away at that moment.

The clock struck 12 and on that beautiful rooftop, she blew out the candles and cut the cake. This was followed by a sweet B 'day song arranged by the hotel staff. It was the perfect place and moment for me to put the next part of my plan into action.

We shared the cake and took some photos although we knew that every single detail of that day would be etched in our memories forever. She responded to the calls and wishes she got from her friends. When we finally had some time left to ourselves again, I asked her to sit down at the table again. And as she did so, the waiter opened a champagne bottle and poured it into a glass for her.

Out popped the final and biggest surprise I had planned for the day. To say that I wasn't nervous would be an understatement.

Till this day I'm yet to come across a day as nervous as that night. I had put the final surprise in my blazer pocket. Inconspicuously I had taken it out and hid it in my palm. As she was relishing the moment and registering the colours of the night, I slowly, without taking my eyes off hers, brought my hand up to the table. With one hand hiding the surprise, I took her hand in my other hand. And was holding her hand by her fingers. When I had a not–so-very-firm grip on her ring finger, she sensed something (she was clever).

Before she could even react, afraid that any words would spoil the sanctity of the moment, I took the ring in my hands and followed with an extempore (This part is not fiction) "This is your birthday but **you** are **my gift**.

I'm not a greedy guy and am not asking for more. Just let me surprise you for the rest of your life. Not just on your birthday. . . But every day. . . I don't want to you to say yes. I don't want you to say no. I am not asking your permission. I am just saying my intention" And with a one more look at her, I put the ring on her finger.

All of you would have probably expected her to fly into my arms and shout out 'YES'. But she simply smiled at me and said "It's complicated. Why don't we talk about it later?" I wouldn't be able to explain in words, how nervous I was till that moment. It was her reply that brought me back to reality. I wasn't really disappointed though, as I never really expected her to reciprocate my feelings. I just took the celebration as an opportunity to show her what I felt about her.

With the plan successfully executed, we drove back to the hostel, but not before enjoying a long drive in the middle of the night (trust me, you got to do this with your better half at least once). All through the drive, she kept on gushing about how excited and surprised she had been that night. I dropped her back at her hostel and drove back to the rental service showroom to return the car. By the time I reached my room, my inbox was filled with her messages.

As I started settling down for the night, my roommates surrounded me, wanting to know how my day went and whether she had accepted my proposal or not. Before I could actually start explaining what happened, my phone rang. It was her, and I grabbed the opportunity to move away from my 'too eager' roommates and talk to her. We spent the entire night talking about the birthday celebration, and her last message I received before she slept of was 'I never expected a birthday like this. You really mean a lot to me'.

I asked her to get some rest, stating that I would pick her up at 8.30 in the morning. As I mentioned before, my plan was to keep surprising her from morning till night the next day.

She asked me to wake her up before sleeping off. And I did just that. I woke her up and asked her to get ready as I went to pick her up in the morning. She didn't even bother to ask me where we were heading this time. She probably knew that whatever I planned, I would plan according to her wishes and likes. Thus started the next phase of my surprise.

I took her to one of the most famous temples in the area and arranged for some puja (religious rituals) to be performed in her name. I had no idea what she prayed for. But I'm sure all of you will know what I probably prayed for in the temple that day.

Following a scrumptious South Indian breakfast at Saravana Bhavan (a hotel that specializes in South Indian vegetarian dishes), we started driving along the East Coast Road, a scenic beach view road from Chennai to Pondicherry.

She loved every minute of her birthday, but was very quiet during the ride. When I asked her the reason for the same, she replied nonchalantly, "I'm tired of your surprises Kiddo.

And I have actually stopped wondering what will come next". I could understand the happiness resonating in her heartbeats, and remained silent for the rest of the trip. Or at least that's what I believed.

The scenic drive was very refreshing and she loved it thoroughly. At the end of it, we entered a beach resort called 'PARK HYAT'. A man looking like a swimming instructor welcomed us and gave us complimentary drinks, asking us to wait while he finished the necessary paperwork for us. I looked at her to see that familiar quizzical expression on her face. She had no idea what was going on, and did not know what to expect as well.

The person who had welcomed us, returned with some papers for us to sign, stating that it was a necessary formality to agree to the terms and conditions, and acknowledge the same by signing the papers.

A couple all alone in a beach resort with someone asking them to sign some papers! You would probably have got some suspicious thoughts about it all by now. Don't fret. What happened is not what you expect at all!

We were given life jackets and guided to the beach. And that's when she saw my next surprise; a catamaran on the beach waiting just for us. Two helpers stood by the boat, waiting for us to board it.

The moment she saw the catamaran, she started jumping up and down in non-stop excitement. It was a long dream of hers to go on a catamaran ride. I had remembered that well enough to arrange this surprise for her. She couldn't control her excitement as we boarded the catamaran (and neither could I) as we headed out to sea.

The first few moments of a catamaran ride is probably the most exhilarating experience you would ever have on a boat ride. Scary and yet exciting, you would clutch hold on to whatever you could with bated breath as the catamaran pushes against the oncoming waves with full force in order to cross them and enter the calmer waters of the sea. For our driver though, it was as simple as switching on a car engine with a key. And after a breathless first few seconds, we headed out to sea.

We stopped about 10 kilometres from the shore. There we were, in the middle of the ocean, just she and I, on her birthday! I opened another cake I had brought along for this very moment and asked her to cut it, wishing her one more time. All this I did, just to make the day the most memorable one in her life.

The cake cut and eaten, we jumped into the sea and spent the next 40 minutes swimming leisurely without a care in the world. Again it was just she and I, surrounded by water and the silent open sky. There was a blissful peace, along with plenty of tears from her end. And as we floated beside each other, our heartbeats resonating with the sound of the waves, it felt as if heaven itself had descended upon us.

When we returned to shore, there was nothing but silence between us. We didn't talk to each other, didn't even want to initiate a conversation, still not having come out of the heavenly experience we had just shared.

We rested below the shade of a few trees, enjoying this moment of silence between us, having no idea of what was running in each other's minds. She was listening to some of her favourite tracks on her iPod while I just lay there beside her with my sunglasses on, staring at the sky which appeared so new suddenly, with an endless streak of bright blue interspersed with white colored clouds. It looked like the perfect canvas, and I marvelled silently at how everything seemed so beautiful when she was with me.

I really don't know how long we lay there in the shade, just minding our own business and not wanting to disturb each other. It was the swimming instructor's voice that brought us back to reality. "So how did it go? Did you guys have fun?"

We packed our things and started walking back to the room that we had booked. After a shower, we headed out for lunch at a nice seafood restaurant. We left the place just before sunset in order to reach her hostel early. And as I dropped her off at her hostel, I finished off my list of birthday surprises by giving her one last gift – a soulful HUG.

The surprise birthday party I had successfully executed earned me a special place in her heart. We started spending more time together after that. Life had turned upside down for me as well. Anything and everything I looked at or heard sounded so gentle and caring. And I got these feelings whenever she was near me or talked to me on the phone.

Even my mobile phone had become like a vital organ of my body which I needed for survival. I couldn't bear to miss even a single text or call from her no matter what.

Her likes, dislikes and wishes became top priority for me. The times we spent together, the places we had visited, all had become very beautiful memories etched in my heart to cherish forever.

Every single day, I started liking her more than the previous day and less than the next one.

One day, while casually chatting on the phone, she remarked that she would be the luckiest girl alive if I happened to become her husband. I didn't know if she mentioned it causally or was pretty serious about what she said. But I took it sportingly, although a part of me screamed for joy inside! And everything between us was going smoothly until the day came when I came to realize the meaning of the word FEAR.

She called me up, asking me to take her to a temple nearby. She was really bothered about something and said that she was very confused, although she didn't mention what it was she was confused about, right away.

AND I COMPROMISED

I was hoping that she would have called me to discuss about my proposal, for nothing else seemed to strike my mind apart from that. So I dressed up in nice, traditional attire and finished all my prayers even before reaching the temple.

She is a big devotee of Lord Shiva. So she wasn't surprised when I took her to a Shiva temple, although she had not visited this particular temple before but had wanted to do so for quite some time now.

After finishing our prayers, we opted to sit down in the temple premises for some time before heading back home. I waited silently for her to start talking, desperate to hear her open up about our relationship. Seriously, at that point, anything that came out of her mouth would have meant a lot to me. So I held my patience and was silent, waiting for her to talk.

She started by saying that her parents had called her the previous night and had approached the subject of marriage. Hearing that doubled by eagerness and excitement. She continued that her parents told her that they were not happy at the prospect of her working in night shifts anymore, and had wanted (or rather, demanded) that she quit the job immediately, and fly back to her hometown.

Honestly speaking, I wasn't against the fact that she needn't continue working in a night shift job anymore. But to just leave the job and fly back immediately? That was a bit unnerving for me.

All sorts of things started moving around in my head. But I still remained silent, because till now, she had not asked my opinion about any of these things. Nor did she give me any hint about wanting me to convince her to stay back and find her a day job in Chennai or talk to her parents about wanting to marry her since they had started looking out for a groom. No, she was talking as though she was just letting out her feelings. And more than her, it was I who was becoming increasingly confused at this juncture.

After spilling out her heart, she sounded a bit ok. And that was that. Without discussing anything else, we walked a few minutes before hiring an auto. On the way back, I slowly initiated the subject of her continuing to stay on in Chennai and search for a day shift job. She didn't respond to my queries at all apart from just nodding her head at everything that I said. And I really didn't know whether she was accepting my words or ignoring them.

I dropped her at the hostel and started back to my room. She called me later to say that she would be visiting another temple alone to clear her head. That left me with practically nothing else to do but worry my head off for the rest of the night. I bought a couple of beer bottles and headed home to my roommates who were more than willing to listen to anything and everything I wanted to let out.

She slept peacefully that night because she had told me everything she wanted me to know. However, judging by the massive hangover I got the next day, I guess my night must have passed eventfully.

Within two days, she had decided to put in her papers and claimed that her parents were really forcing her to do so. In fact, I took the ultimate honour of drafting her resignation email after she asked me to do so and I was left with no other option but to oblige. She sent the resignation mail to the management the very next day, stating the reason as 'higher studies'.

All this while, I kept talking to her, trying to find out what she exactly thought about me and my proposal. I knew she was her dad's princess and would not do anything against his wish. She asked me to come and talk to her dad about asking her hand in marriage. However, she did not encourage me with any words of hope which I was desperate to hear.

And though she indirectly admitted her wish to marry me more than once, she only spoke of the hindrances that remained in our paths. It wasn't any new reason that no one had heard of before, but the usual "ifs and buts" that accompany every love relationship, different castes, different languages, different states, her parent's opposition to love marriages and so on……..

The good thing about all this is that she didn't deny me a chance to try to talk to her dad and convince him to agree to our marriage. However, she made it clear that no matter what happens, she shouldn't be blamed at the end of it all.

I really don't know why many girls actually do this to the guy they love. How could they keep their likes and wishes buried inside their hearts and act as if nothing had happened? I have seen girls who contradict the fact that girls are not weaker than boys, by claiming that they can do whatever boys can do. However, when it comes to handling a situation like this, all these girls back out at the last minute, saying they can't hurt their parents in the process of fighting for their love, and that the same love they were ready to die for at one point of time, is not worth their parent's tears. Of course, I do understand that you can't hurt your parents in any way possible, especially in love. My question then is, why bother to love at all?

Anyways, I knew we wouldn't be able to derive a possible solution for the situation we were in currently by just talking about it for hours on end. I decided to give the whole matter some time and space, and started preparing myself mentally to meet her parents and talk to them about our marriage. Time was a very important factor in this matter, and I wanted to get the perfect opportunity to speak to them.

However, before that, I needed to face my parents first. I know my parents very well, and knew at that point that it would take all the courage I had built up over the years to stand in front of them and tell them that I liked a girl and wanted to marry her.

The fact that both of us (especially I) were still too young for marriage also made me hesitate a bit about talking to both her parents as well as my parents.

During the last thirty days of her stay in Chennai, I wanted to spend every single moment of my time with her. However, a mail at work one day diverted all the thoughts buzzing around in our heads at that time.

It was about a dance competition between several corporate companies for a social cause. And I was given the responsibility of winning the competition on behalf my company.

It was her wish as well that I should win the competition, and that she could watch me dance one last time before leaving town. That alone was enough for me to agree to it even though I knew the dance was planned for another special reason, a social cause.

More than anybody, she knew what dance meant to me. She had witnessed the pleasure and pride plastered on my face whenever I danced. And she had told me many times that she was my first and biggest fan. That made it all the more special, and I set my heart on winning the competition for her.

I assembled a team of dancers from the company and we started practicing. We had eighteen days left for the competition. And there were still twenty two days left for her to leave town for good.

The first few days of dance practice were vague. I needed a lot of effort to mentor the team, as all of us were corporate employees and not professional dancers. A lot of confusion lingered among us as to what song to select, what costumes to wear, what kind of performance to give and so on.

Through various sources from other companies (mostly friends of friends), we heard that other dance teams in these places had already appointed renowned dance choreographers and had started their practice in full swing.

I never have any serious thoughts when it comes to winning a competition. I never really do. All I do is believe in myself and enjoy what I am doing (in this case, dancing). And that, according to me, always provided me with better results.

While at practice one day, I received a call from her. It was some time in the afternoon, and I could easily guess that something was wrong the moment I heard her voice at the other end. She was almost in tears. My heart started pounding in fear as I started envisioning something really bad. in a scared voice. I asked her what had happened. And in a broken voice, she asked me if I could do her a big favour.

In spite of being scared, I got a bit confused now, wondering what would've made her cry. The words came instantly out of my mouth though, "Anything for you. Tell me what I can do".

In the same broken voice, she replied "I want you to win this dance competition no matter what". She continued "I have never asked you for anything from the time I met you. But now, the winning moment of this competition is all that I wish from you".

The only reaction my mind could take was "WHAT??? Is that all that she wanted? That's like eating ice cream for me". I was pretty confused that this simple wish had set her crying, but kept my thoughts to myself and accepted her request without any questions. After all, it was for her. But I could guess that ultimately, she wanted me to win the competition so that everyone in the office (even those who belittle me) would be proud of me.

Her only wish compounded my reasons to win this dance competition, come what may. I put my heart and soul into it, and spent days and nights focussed on our performance. I started choreographing the routine while envisioning myself dancing on stage, with her watching me from the audience. That increased my enthusiasm and I gave it everything that I had, only for her.

We didn't bother about our conversations which had reduced quite a bit, for I was busy with the practice sessions and had dedicated most of my time for it and other tasks related to the competition.

It didn't even occur to me that one single day in between all this could bring such a gap between us. She got a call from her parents asking her to fly down to her hometown exactly a week before the competition.

She told me that it was for just a day and that she would return the very next day. I didn't mind not asking her the reason for this urgent visit and remained tight lipped even while dropping her off at the airport.

She kept me posted till the time she reached her home. The last message I received from her mobile was that she would be right back as her parents wanted to talk about something important, and that she wouldn't be able to text me during their conversation. I attached my mobile to the charging unit and continued my dance practice.

A few hours later, as I was packing my stuff to head home, she texted me, asking me what I was doing and whether I had had my dinner.

I texted back saying that I was just about to start for home after completing the dance practice session. I followed it up with a casual query 'Is all well back there?' Her reply was quick 'Nothing to worry'.

Both of us didn't extend our conversation beyond that as she was at home. I also believed that if something serious or important had happened there, she would have definitely informed me, or at least, let me know. Her last message came in the night when she wished me good night, stating that she had to catch the return flight early in the morning the next day. We signed of early in the night, a first ever in our entire chatting history.

I couldn't go to the airport the next morning to pick her up as I had to pick up my parents who had arrived at Chennai suddenly on for some work. The only thing running in my mind the entire time was how great it would be if I could take this opportunity to introduce her to my parents, and probably lay the foundation stone for letting them know about our marriage plans.

I invited my parents to the dance competition and they agreed without hesitation. That added more fuel to my excitement of participating and winning the competition, especially since I would be dancing for her. And also because this would be the first time my parents would see me dancing on a stage. I knew the time had come for me to make them proud and let them know what dance really meant to me.

The next few days were spent in work, practice and spending time with my parents. I hardly could manage to find some time to talk to her. And she didn't bother me with her regular calls and non-stop messages either. That felt a bit weird, but I refrained from asking her whether something was bothering her as she was not talking properly to me those days.

But come what may, I never used to miss the opportunity of walking with her from the office to her hostel after work every day. Those few minutes of quality time with her defined my day. Her hostel was located less than a kilometre from the office. I usually waited for her on the steps of a shop (it would obviously be closed at that hour) located around eight hundred meters from the office so that no one would be able to notice us.

Her shift would end by 6.00am in the morning and I usually reached the waiting spot before 5.30am. The place was notorious for mosquitoes. And I served as food and entertainment for these mosquitoes every morning until she would leave the building and reach our waiting spot.

She had, in fact, scolded me many times for waiting in that mosquito ridden area. But she loved the morning walk we shared every day, and probably thought that was a small price I had to pay for the same.

That day, I conveyed my apologies to her, stating that I would not be able to spend more time with her owing to my parent's visit.

I had noticed that she had not been her usual self for the past few days. Something was really bothering her, but she was keeping mum about it. She knew very well that I didn't have the habit of forcing people into doing things they don't like or are hesitant about. And she used this trait of mine to her advantage, choosing to remain silent and withdrawn while I wondered what was running in her mind.

It was the day before the competition, and we had finally concluded our practice session. I decided to allot every individual his/her responsibilities in order to avoid last minute hassles and mess-ups.

The team decided to go and hire the costumes in the evening. So I hurried up for a quick meeting with her before she started office for the day. I informed her that I would not be able to join her for our customary morning walk the next morning as I was going to stay at a friend's place that night in order to complete pending computer work.

I was overexcited about the next day's event, and asked her to make sure and take leave. She informed me that she had already applied for leave, stating that her parents had come to town to visit her. At that time, I didn't know that the reason she had given was not fake, but real.

I chatted with her for a few minutes before heading off to hire the costumes for the dance.

I didn't receive her regular calls or text messages during her breaks that day. Being pre-occupied about her, my mind was full of worries about what had happened to her and whether something was bothering her. The thoughts started disturbing my mind as we finished hiring the costumes and headed over to my friend's house for the night. With just a night remaining for the dance, my mind was crowding over with thoughts of how to win the competition rather than concentrating on her, even though I felt she was avoiding talking to me for some reason.

Settling down in my friend's home, I started planning out the events for the next day's performance. My body was too tired to cope with my rather active mind. Surprisingly, my friend supported me this time (he would usually challenge my abilities) by staying up with me and making sure my head remained clear of obtrusions.

We had planned on a ten minute dance routine that would incorporate different dancing styles (they called it a fusion in those days). Hip hop was a top priority for any dance completion but, I so badly wanted to add to my routine.

However, my team comprised of corporate employees and I couldn't expect them to do a standard hip hop routine just like that. Therefore, in spite of knowing that some of the choreographers for other companies were making (or rather, forcing) their teams to practice hip hop routines, I decided for a 'freestyle' dance routine with some attractive moves that would look almost like hip hop.

I had to make all the necessary arrangements that night itself. I started editing the songs we would need for the performance, and followed it up by working on the moviemaker software to create the film certificate and bloopers we planned on adding to our performance.

It was nearing 11.30 p.m. and I was expecting her to call or at least message me. Nothing. I finally managed to get hold of her on the phone by around 2.00 in the morning. Luckily, it was her coffee break and she picked up my call. With a disturbed mind and very heavy heart, I told her that I was finding it difficult to concentrate on my work since she had not called me the entire day and was not responding properly.

She replied quite bluntly that her parents were visiting her the next morning and that she would not be able to be a part of the show as she had to spend time with them.

Do I need any other reason to get very upset? Nope, I don't think so. And after that very awful conversation, she disconnected my call and went back to work.

By this time, I was more than upset and disturbed. My friend seemed to notice it, and took me out for a smoke. I explained everything to him, stating how hard it was for me to accept that she would not be a part of the event the next day. My friend tried his best to convince me, but I was inconsolable. After two cigarettes, we headed inside to notice that my laptop had switched off automatically.

I hoped that it might have been due to low charge.

I connected the charger to the laptop before trying to switch it on again. Nothing.

After struggling with it for a few minutes, we decided to hit the bed and think about it the next morning rather than stay up all night and break our heads trying to find out what had happened.

I woke up the next morning, full of anticipation at the thoughts of winning the competition for her.

I looked at my cell phone. Disappointment.

Not even a single call or message from her.

With such a disappointing start to an otherwise promising day, I walked up to my laptop and tried to switch it on, only to discover that the operating system in my laptop had crashed completely, meaning, all the work I had done and saved in it was gone for ever.

I started to panic, but my friend reassured me by saying that we still had time till evening to figure out something. We headed for the office as that was where we had planned to meet the rest of the team that morning.

Firstly, no phone calls or messages from her. And now this. Too many things started bothering my mind at the same time at this juncture and I started to wonder whether it would really be worth it to dance in the competition if she was not there to watch me.

My troubled state of mind might have just rubbed off on my teammates as well before I even arrived. With her not being there for the event and my laptop crashing, I was wondering what else could make the day worse when, upon entering the office, I saw my teammates sitting separately in different areas of the room, not talking to each other, as if something really bad had happened.

I started explaining about the laptop crash the previous night and how I had lost all the stuff I had edited, when my teammates silenced me, wanting me to listen to bigger, more serious problems.

Apparently, a few girls in the team had not liked the costumes that I had ordered for them. As they started raising their voice against me, I watched them silently, fuming in frustration.

After a few seconds, every one jumped in with his/her share of problems regarding the dance performance. There were hardly two hours left for the performance and we were asked to report to the auditorium. Did they had to come up with all these problems only now?

That was it! I lost my cool and lambasted them for not opening their mouths the previous day when we had gone to hire the costumes. It was then that I realized that I had been too preoccupied about her the previous evening to understand or even notice what my teammates had been telling me. The truth was, I had not paid full attention to the proceedings the previous evening.

I quietly walked away from the place and sat down to smoke. By the time I had finished the second cigarette, my mind had cleared (and calmed down) enough to make me try and talk to my teammates about continuing with the performance anyway. But they were adamant. They wanted a new set of costumes and that was it!

I couldn't believe that in an hour, we had gone through almost nine sets of costumes until we zeroed in on the ones that EVERYONE liked!

Without any time for lunch, we rushed straight to the auditorium, and thankfully, reported on time (you get disqualified if you don't). A green room was allotted to us for dressing and makeup. I quickly sat down to work on the song recording again. And I still have no idea how I got the brainstorm of using MS Office PowerPoint to make the movie clips I had earlier lost in my laptop.

As I was getting ready for the performance, I got a call from her, asking me what I was doing. I tried to convince her to visit the auditorium along with her parents. She replied that she couldn't, but said that she would call me back at 6 in the evening. She also asked me not to contact her in between till she call me again after reaching the hostel. Saying that, she disconnected the call.

As time passed and the competition drew nearer, the seats in the auditorium started filling up with employees of different organizations along with their friends and family members. We got into our costumes, me ever so slowly, because of the fact that she was not coming that day and I had no other reason to perform. And that's when my parents showed up. Their appearance put a smile back up on my face and I consoled myself saying that at least my parents had turned up. I went backstage to get a quick blessing from them and joined my teammates to wait for the performance.

Lots were drawn to see which team would perform first. And not surprisingly, our team was asked to perform first. Judging from all that had happened from that morning up until the last few minutes before the competition, I knew that God had helped me sort things out, and thanked Him for the same. And as we got on to the stage to perform, everything fell into place.

The opening credits flew by and the curtains opened to a deafening response from the audience and then the music started. The audience went mad and the whoops, yells and screams continued until we ended the performance. The last folk song in particular literally set the stage on fire and resulted in quite a few encores being thrown our way from the audience.

Our scintillating performance finished, we decided to continue with the celebration and joined the audience for some more fun and dance. It also gave us a chance to see how our competitors were performing.

Sadly, every team was exceptional. And after every single performance, our hopes of winning the coveted trophy would either increase or decrease. We started praying for a chance to win the trophy especially when the last dance began, a theme based performance which left the audience, including me, awestruck.

After the performances were all over, we were asked to gather by the side of the stage for the results. I couldn't imagine losing the competition. Dance had been everything to me, and still was everything to me as I discovered during the past few days. It was all I knew and all I was extremely good at. I started praying fervently to God, asking Him to bless me that day.

The event concluded, the judges came up on stage to announce the results.

We waited with bated breath and I was so tense I could actually feel my heart stop beating for a second. The decision of the judges was unanimous, as they said. And as they opened the envelope to reveal the winner, everything around me paused, as if in a freeze mode. At that moment, I missed the presence of another heart that was expecting me to lift the trophy.

And then there it was! The results everyone, especially I was tersely waiting for. The same results for which I had spent sleepless days and nights for the past couple of weeks. The results she had dreamed of and which I knew was my gift for her; the 1st place in the Group Dance Event!

Photos were taken with the trophy, hugs were shared between teammates, and compliments and wishes flooded us non-stop from everyone around us. My parents were actually amused at all the appreciation coming my way. And yet, they were very happy that they had finally witnessed me dance, and had realized what dance really meant to me.

Everyone was living that moment with so many celebrations and so much happiness. I did not feel like taking part in any of it though. My heart was crying out for her, missing her presence at the event, silently crying out over the fact that she had missed my proud moment, the moment she had wished and asked me for. But I decided against making it a big issue for I thought that there might definitely be a serious reason behind her not turning up at the event or calling me.

Another thing that kept nagging me was the fact that I couldn't call or text her to reveal the results of the competition right away as she had specifically instructed me not to text or call her until she came back to the hostel (she had gone out somewhere with her parents, and I hadn't minded not asking her where).

Pushing all these worries to the back of my mind, I decided to celebrate our victory that night at my friend's place again. I dropped my parents at a relative's place and headed over to his house with some beers. I would have stopped my bike at least 50 times in between to check for her missed call or message. Nothing!!!!

Downing a few beers, I waited for her call. My impatience got the better of me when, at 11.30 in the night, I couldn't wait any longer and decided to call her against all her instructions.

More than a surprise, it was a complete shock for me when she answered her phone half asleep. Here I was, waiting up all night for at least one call or message from her, and there she was sleeping peacefully, not even wanting to know how the competition had gone and how we had fared in it. It was a 'heartbreak' moment, if you want to know exactly how I felt at that moment. I was completely disappointed and let down. And what followed next did not lift up my spirits any more.

She nonchalantly said that she was too tired to talk and whether we could speak the next morning. My patience running out, I demanded a few minutes of conversation, stating that it was really important that I talk to her right then.

She asked me what it was, as if she didn't have an iota of thought of what I was about to tell her.

Her indifference didn't deter me, for at that instant, I forgot everything as I exclaimed with equal pride and excitement "Hey Honey (yes, I used to call her that). You asked me something and here we go ---- I DID IT. I won the dance competition. And I dedicated my winning moment to you".

"Oh, congratulations." That's all she said.

Let me ask you something here. How would you react to such a response? If you could answer this question in your minds, then you would probably realize how I felt at that moment. Coming from my mouth though, that was a completely WTF moment, for I clearly could feel that she was not in the least bit excited on hearing the news.

I asked her, ever so politely, "Hey, what's wrong with you? Aren't you excited or happy like I am at winning the competition? This is what you wanted from me, right?"

Her very casual reply further tore at my heart as she coolly commented that she knew from the start that I would win the competition at any cost, which is why she was neither surprised nor excited to hear the results.

I just stood there, not knowing what to speak. After a really long breath, all that could come out of my mouth was "Okay. Thank you".

"Mmmmmmmmm", she replied.

And that was it. That blew my lid and I demanded to know why she had been avoiding me for the past one week. I forced her to talk to me about whatever was bothering her mind, stating that I felt really weird that she was acting that way with me.

Finally, after what seemed like ages, she decided to open her mouth. And that, was a moment that I still wish had never happened in my life, a moment I could turn back to and stop from happening, a moment that remains fresh in my heart even if I try erasing it from my mind.

She revealed that the reason her parents had come down urgently for a day's visit to the city was to arrange a marriage proposal for her. She continued that her father had been adamant about the proposal and had gone ahead and finalized it.

With a cracking voice, she continued, stating that the reason why she had not been able to attend the competition was because her mom and dad had visited her along with the groom and his family. The icing on the cake came when she claimed that she had almost got engaged that day as their families had completed the initial rituals of exchanging vows to confirm everything.

Now, if you were expecting me to react in a mature way and take things lightly, then you are very wrong. I didn't do any of that. Instead, I cried out and started screaming at her (excuse me; I was drunk at that time).

When I asked her why she hadn't told me about these developments earlier, she sobbed back with an excuse that made me take back those words I had mentioned earlier about her excuse for not calling or texting me earlier ----- 'there might definitely be a serious reason behind her not turning up at the event or calling me'.

The reason? The answer she gave was one of the stupidest reasons I could think of to avoid someone. She mentioned that she was worried that if I had come to know about all this, I would have given up on the competition and not concentrated properly on the dance, and failed to win. Seriously, couldn't she have come up with a better reason than that? I felt angry, bewildered and utterly helpless by her words.

What she said next mellowed me down a bit though. In between sobs, she claimed that she had just gone through the worst seven days of her life by not telling me what had happened, trying to get out of the situation she was in herself.

At that moment, my anger vanished and a more serious emotion, worry (and fear) started settling in. And from that moment onwards, my fear of losing her started clouding my judgment on anything and everything around me.

She told me that she had enough time to convince her parents in order to buy herself some time, and that relaxed me a bit.

However, something still kept nagging my mind.

Throughout all this, I could see that while my only fear was 'losing her', her only fear was about 'getting married' --- not to me or anyone else --- because according to her, I was still a Best Friend she would rely on and share anything and everything at any time.

The next few days passed like mere seconds, and the day came when she finished her thirty day notice period and had to leave the city to go back home. The thought of missing her was driving me crazy day by day. When she was around, everything looked beautiful and cheerful to me. But after she left, everything turned upside down. I had never felt so lonely in my life, and literally hated every second of it the next few days. I couldn't eat, sleep, breathe, work ---- nothing! It was like I was getting a taste of what hell was like while I was still alive and walking.

She was cool however, because she had understood the situation perfectly. Rather, she had accepted the fact that sooner or later she would have to marry the groom her father chose for her. And she felt that since she was going to be at home, it would be all the more feasible for her parents to convince her for the marriage. And that thought of hers gave me more sleepless nights.

A month passed by with her not calling me and with me trying to find out the exact moment to correct this unnerving situation I had landed in. That was when, one fine day, she called me from home to talk casually, rather complain about how she didn't want to get married to a complete stranger.

I took this as my cue and started trying to convince her to marry me instead, claiming how I much loved her, cared for and wanted to marry her. At one point, I believed she also started to think seriously about my proposal, for she didn't respond negatively as she had done the previous times. She just remained quiet at the other end, listening to me. And that sounded as if she wanted me to get her out of the situation, as if she was asking me 'Do something na, baba'.

Another day, while we were talking over SKYPE, she shared what her mother had asked her the previous night whether she was ready to marry the guy they had chosen, and revealed that she had not known how to react to it. Neither did I. She continued, stating that her mother had asked her to take her own time to think about the marriage, and that they weren't forcing her to get married right away. Apparently, she wanted her to spend more time with the groom and talk to him more frequently in order to get to know him better, just like she talks with me.

Those last words jolted me back to reality and I suddenly realized what had to be done. I had to talk to her parents and convince them for her hand in marriage. I started by convincing her first, stating that her mother must have uttered those words either because she knew we were in a relationship, or because she had a huge amount of respect for our friendship.

My eagerness for that exact moment to talk to her parents coupled with my fear of losing her did not let me hesitate from wanting to fly down to her hometown immediately. I told her that I would come down to talk to her parents as soon as possible.

If, at that point, she was not interested in my proposal, she could easily have said NO. But she didn't.

That's when a glimmer of hope started shining in my heart. Maybe, just maybe, she was interested in marrying me too, but couldn't stand up against her parents trust in her. And I kind of respected her feelings, as she was just like most of the other girls I had come across who did not want to hurt their parents feelings when it comes to love. Remember? I'm not a male chauvinistic.

I managed to get her address and boarded the flight the very next day, hopeful of happy ending to the harrowing moments I had experienced for the past few days and of a new beginning with her in my life, as my beloved wife.

It took her a few minutes to recover from the shock and surprise of my sudden visit. She hadn't thought that I would land there the very next day itself and reach her home.

I was damn hungry. She managed to cook a dish which she had recently learnt from her mother (girls in India are required to know how to cool before stepping into their In-laws' house). I sat in her bedroom while she cooked, just going through the moment, envisioning myself as being in her home as her father's son in law.

After eating the dish she fondly named after cooking it, we sat down to talk. I mentally prepared myself to face her parents and convince them, especially her dad about my love for her as I really didn't want to, or could not imagine missing her ever.

By the time her parents arrived after work, we were both ready, as he had called me before to confirm our dinner plan.

She asked me to wear a white coloured Chinese collar shirt with mild khaki coloured trousers, and asked me to sport a clean shaven face in order to impress her parents; rather, she wanted to introduce me to her parents that way.

Her father looked very professional and I could tell that he wore a blazer to work every day. Her mother would fit the role of a school teacher perfectly, but was a client service manager in a corporate company. Before leaving for the hotel, I offered a silent prayer to God to bless me with the strength and the correct choice of words I would need to use in order to convince her dad that night.

We had a beautiful dinner, like a loving family. Her parents were very friendly folks and interacted with me as if they knew me from childhood. That really helped me overcome my fear of speaking to them about my relationship with their daughter.

Before leaving the hotel, her dad went to make a call. As he was speaking on the phone, I took her aside and asked her just one question.

"If your dad calls you and asks whether you like me the same as I like you and whether you want to get married to me, will you say yes?"

As usual, she remained silent. If she had said to me that night or at least told her dad what I wanted to hear, life would have been a whole lot different for me now, and I wouldn't be talking to you about all the things I compromised in my life.

We boarded the cab to head back home. And that is when I decided to open my mouth and tell her parents everything I had in mind.

Throughout my conversation with them, she remained silent and withdrawn; as if guilty that she had known what it is I had come to Mumbai for, but did not have the guts to tell them herself.

I chose my words carefully, making sure I explained about our relationship properly without making him feel bad or cheated upon by his daughter, his princess. And through all this, the only weapon I had with me and which gave me the confidence to go on was her word, "Yes". The word she said she would use if her father decided to ask her all those questions I said he would ask.

He dropped me at the hotel and said that his daughter would call me and tell me about his response soon. He wished me a safe journey back and left.

The four hours I spent in the hotel after that had me thinking a lot of things. I kept asking myself "What am I doing here? Is what I am doing right?" However, I knew that I would not regret that moment for anything, for I wouldn't have to get up one day and say that I didn't try.

But one thing made me more nervous and panicky than everything else. Her father's response. I kept on waiting for her call the entire night, hoping to hear something, anything that could at least give me a glimmer of hope about a future with her. Nothing. I boarded the flight back home in the morning, all the while checking my mobile for her call or message. I got nothing till I reached Chennai.

Her father called me a couple of days later. And this is what he had to say, "She is not interested in your proposal. You can still be her friend if you remove all those thoughts about her from your head. If not, better leave her alone and stop talking to her".

AND I COMPROMISED

Although his words were harsh, he spoke politely and repeated the words so as to make me understand his stance as a father in all this; as if he wanted me to stand in his shoes and think about these events. And that was it. I knew at that moment that she had failed me at that exact point where I had wanted her to hold my hand and stand her ground.

Days and months passed by. Our daily conversations were reduced drastically as she started preparing herself mentally to marry the guy of her dad's choice. During this period, I made all the possible attempts, including sending her plenty of emails and messages to let her know about my feeling for her. However, every time I moved a bit forward, she pushed me back saying "This cannot happen". I could see that she was not prepared to go against her father's wishes even in her dreams. Most of these email/text conversations often ended with my crying, thinking, rather fearing, that I was ultimately going to lose her.

After plenty of struggles in dealing with this rather complicated situation of mine, I decided for the first time to compromise. That didn't mean I gave up entirely. Rather, I thought I would try one last time. I decided to hit her where it would hurt most, her emotions, so that at least then she would understand my love for her.

I decided to send her an email as my last weapon to let her know how mad I was about her, and how, without her, I had no life. At that moment, I never realized or even thought about the fact that my first ever conversation with her started with an email, and that my last conversation with her would be via an email as well.

It was December 16th, our first year anniversary, the day I had my first ever conversation with her. And this is what my email had to say.

(If you can then imagine an email that would make your heart pound, throat thicken with something you can't absolutely swallow. My email was rather like that)

From: XXXX@XX.COM

To: XXXX@XX.COM
Subject: DON'T LIKE TO MENTION A SUBJECT.
Date: Dec 16th / 01:03 AM.

Hey,

Just wanted to send you an email about everything that's going on in my mind for the past few days. This may possibly be my last chance to let you know what I feel too.

I preferred talking to you via email and then I realized that this would actually complete the circle: our relationship (or whatever it was) is going to end the same way it started – by an email!

The memory of that first email I sent you still remains fresh in my mind. It was our very first conversation. And in the days to come, I'll remember this one too, embedded like a stone carving in my heart.

To tell you the truth, it was very hard for me to accept the fact; that all these days it was only I who had had these thoughts of us being in a relationship. You had not talked about it or even hinted about it at any point. I understand now that, all along, I was thinking only about myself: what *I* wanted and how *I* wanted you to be in my life.

Maybe you would have felt better (and happier) if I had taken you to the restaurant of your choice or your favourite chaat shop on your birthday. You never wished for surprises. It was I who showered them on you. I now understand things clearly from your point of view. While I was fervently developing feelings for you, I realize now that there was nothing from your side, not then, and not now as well. And I finally understand how unfair it had been of me to force you to feel about me the same way I felt about you.

Yes, I realize that I am a victim of the notorious one-sided love.

I was thinking of every convincing reason to put forth to your dad, if at all he were to say NO to my proposal. Foreseeing every question and preparing an answer. And

I did, in fact, put a couple of convincing points when he had called me yesterday. Until what he said made sense to me: He never said that he wasn't interested. He was trying to tell me that YOU were not interested!

I used to debate with myself telling "If a good couple can be good friends, why can't two good friends make a great couple!" But it is only after the meeting with your father I realised that you never wished for the latter!

Well. Bygones be bygones. Many people feel that something is always better than nothing. But for me it was either everything or nothing. And I ended up with …. You know it.

I would rather break off once and for all rather than pretend to be a friend to the girl I love the most. Coz it's better to kill yourself for once rather than keep stabbing yourself in the heart every single day.

To say that you will be remembered in every sunset and sunrise of my life would be an understatement! Because YOU are my sunset and sunrise.

And yes! Hope you remember, today is our first Anniversary!! Happy Anniversary ☺ (Don't ask me for what)

Yours.
XXXXX…

She called and cried a loud that night after she read my mail.

It's been more than two years since I sent her that mail. She stopped talking to me very abruptly after my last mail. And I have not spoken to her since.

In spite of sending her that mail and having every intention of sticking to whatever I had said in it, I couldn't control myself from talking to her the very next day. But she did what I could not do. She stopped responding to my calls, messages and mails.

I tried every possible way to contact her again, except visiting her again. I must have sent more than 10000 messages and nearly millions of calls through phone, Facebook and even Skype, but nothing helped.

I even tried contacting her previous roommate (the one who had helped me out with those gifts) but received the same response: to leave her alone and not bother her anymore.

The pain of not talking to someone you are crazy about and accepting the fact that she doesn't want to talk to you isn't easy to explain and is unbearable.

However, unlike other guys around me, I never tried growing a beard, sporting a gloomy face, drinking uncontrollably or cutting off all contacts from the real world. Nope. I was heartbroken, but I never felt like doing all these things to prove that I had lost someone that I dearly loved. It took me four whole months to come out of that terrible pain. And then, one day ......

I decided to sit down and start writing about everything I had ever compromised in life, without actually knowing where to start and where to end.

After more than two years of not being in contact with each other, one weekend in Bangalore, I was spending time with my friends. And that's when I got a hunch on how to finish my story.

It was a busy evening on MG Road. I was enjoying a walk with my friends. All of a sudden, we entered a Health and Glow Shop, and after spending a few minutes inside with my friends, I decided to come outside for some fresh air.

The marriage function for which I had come to Bangalore in the first place had taken a toll on my body. I was completely exhausted after two sleepless nights, and wished to just hit my bed once I reached home and sleep for as long as I could.

I was resting outside the shop, watching people who past me. Just as I turned back, I noticed someone coming out of the shop. I expected it to be one of my friends, but it was not any of them that I saw there.

For a moment, time froze as we looked at each other, shocked, surprised and utterly blanked out…. Until she said "Hi, what are you doing here?"

Now don't go about getting any ideas. For it was not she that I met, but her friend, the hostel mate. And surprisingly, she wasn't rude enough to just walk away from me as if she didn't know me.

I told her about my weekend visit to arrange a friend's wedding, following which, we had a very quick formal conversation. Finally, after just a few seconds of chit chat, she said 'See you around' and started to walk away.

I bid adieu to her and returned to the same position I had been in before noticing her. As she started going down the stairs, my curiosity got the better of me and I called out to her. And she stopped immediately and turned around, as if she knew I would call her to ask her what I wanted to ask.

"Hey, just wanted to know. How is she doing and where is she now?

Is she married?"

She responded "…………………………..:

And then I realized that this time it wasn't me, it's she who had compromised.

Compromise – Is not a Planned Failure.

It's not about knowing something; it's about realizing it, even though it hurts you. And with time, I learned to realize the fact that some people do stay in your hearts for ever, but can never be a part of your life.

For all those guys who act and do crazy things for their queens, their 'Dad's Princesses'; MAY GOD SAVE YOU.

And for all those daughters who want to make their parents proud by accepting their choice of grooms and families; MAY GOD BLESS YOU.

After all, if it's not for your parents and family, who else can you, compromise for. All that you are now is because of them. And you owe them big time for that. That's what I have come to realize along the way, that compromise is not a bad thing, especially if you do it for someone like your parents. It may tug at your heart at times and you would always have that question lingering in your mind, 'What If?' However, when you look back at them a few years down the lane, you would know why it was better this way.

I have never had any regrets in my life till date because I strongly believe in the saying 'Life is not about what you couldn't do so far. Rather, it's about what you can still do.'

Every one of you reading this book would have compromised on your dreams, passions and more importantly, your love at one point of time or the other. All I want to say to you is 'Chill out. I have been there and done that. It's not the end of your life if you didn't get what you wanted. And life doesn't always have to end if you don't achieve your dreams, passion or that loved one you lost.

If my attempt at being a writer doesn't bear fruit, I will just add it to the list of all the other compromises I had made in my life, including basketball, dance and love; and will keep on going. After all, life has to move on no matter what.

But one thing! No one, absolutely no one, can take away these memories from you. They will live within you, a part of your soul and only come to the forefront when you come across something that reminds you of those past wonderful moments.

At such moment, it would be wonderful if there is someone with whom you can share your feelings.

I will definitely feel my story has been a success if any of the moments mentioned in this book have made you smile, cry or recollect old, wonderful memories of the things that you compromised in life.

Here's to a wonderful life!!

Printed in the United States
By Bookmasters